# Amazing Nature

# Home Makers

## Matt Turner

Heinemann Library
Chicago, Illinois

Customer Service 888-454-2279
Visit our website at www.heinemannlibrary.com

Produced for Heinemann Library by Discovery Books Limited
Originated by Ambassador Litho Ltd
Printed in China by South China Printing Company

08 07 06 05 04
10 9 8 7 6 5 4 3 2 1

**Library of Congress Cataloging-in-Publication Data**
Turner, Matt, 1964-
 Home makers / Matt Turner.
    p. cm. -- (Amazing nature)
Summary: Describes some of the more unusual homes that animals make to protect themselves from harsh weather, hide from predators, and provide a safe nursery for babies.
Includes bibliographical references (p.   ) and index.
 ISBN 1-4034-4705-5 (Hardcover) -- ISBN 1-4034-5401-9 (pbk.)
 1.  Animals--Habitations--Juvenile literature. [1. Animals--Habitations.]  I. Title. II. Series.
 QL756.T885 2003
 591.56'4--dc22

                              2003022041

**Acknowledgments**
The publisher would like to thank the following for permission to reproduce photographs:
p. 4 Franco Banfi/Bruce Coleman Collection; p. 5 Photodisc; p. 6 Kevin Schafer/Natural History Photographic Agency; p. 7 Michael Pitts/Oxford Scientific Films; p. 8 A N T/Natural History Photographic Agency; p. 9 Morten Strange/Natural History Photographic Agency; p. 10 Albert Visage/FLPA; p. 11 Dave Watts/Natural History Photographic Agency; p. 12 Nigel J. Dennis/Natural History Photographic Agency; p. 13 Kjell Sandved/Oxford Scientific Films; p. 14 Kjell Sandved/Oxford Scientific Films; p. 15 Max Gibbs/Oxford Scientific Films; p. 16 Vivek Sinha/SAL/Oxford Scientific Films; p. 17A Winfried Wisniewski/FLPA; p. 17B Tim Jackson/Oxford Scientific Films; p. 18 Luiz Claudio Marigo/Bruce Coleman Collection; p. 19 John Shaw/Natural History Photographic Agency; p. 20 Mantis Wildlife Films/Oxford Scientific Films; p. 21A Mantis Wildlife Films/Oxford Scientific Films; p. 21B E & D Hosking/FLPA; p. 22 Minden Pictures/FLPA; p. 23 Ron Austing/FLPA; p. 24 Dan Griggs/Natural History Photographic Agency; p. 25 Nigel J Dennis/Natural History Photographic Agency; p. 26 Karl Switak/Natural History Photographic Agency; p. 27 Mantis Wildlife Films/Oxford Scientific Films; p. 28 Dave Watts/Natural History Photographic Agency; p. 29 B. Borrell Casals/FLPA.

Cover photograph of a masked weaver: Tim Jackson/Oxford Scientific Films.

Every effort has been made to contact copyright holders of any material reproduced in this book. Any omissions will be rectified in subsequent printings if notice is given to the publisher.

Some words are shown in bold, **like this.** You can find out what they mean by looking in the glossary.

# Contents

A Safe Place to Hide . . . . . . . . . . . . . . . . .4

Simple Refuges . . . . . . . . . . . . . . . . . . . .6

Pack Your Trunk . . . . . . . . . . . . . . . . . . .8

Born in a Bank . . . . . . . . . . . . . . . . . .10

Holes in the Ground . . . . . . . . . . . . . .12

Home Share . . . . . . . . . . . . . . . . . .14

Stitch and Thatch . . . . . . . . . . . . . . .16

Make It with Mud . . . . . . . . . . . . . . .18

Paper and Glue . . . . . . . . . . . . . . . .20

Underground Societies . . . . . . . . . . . .22

Building Big . . . . . . . . . . . . . . . . .24

Homes in Harsh Places . . . . . . . . . . . .26

Fact File . . . . . . . . . . . . . . . . . . . .28

Glossary . . . . . . . . . . . . . . . . . . .30

More Books to Read . . . . . . . . . . . . .31

Index . . . . . . . . . . . . . . . . . . . . .32

# A Safe Place to Hide

Why do animals build homes? Like humans, some animals need to protect themselves from the hot sun, cold wind, rain, or snow. Most animals also need to hide from hunters that would like to eat them. A home can also make a cosy, safe nursery for their young.

Scientists like to discover how an animal knows how to build. A young beaver watches its parents building a **dam,** and is eager to join in. It learns from watching life. A queen hornet, however, has no such teachers. She simply knows how to mold mouthfuls of mashed wood into a nest. Knowledge like this is called **instinct**. Most animals are guided by a mixture of learning and instinct.

*The large, hairy hermit crab lives up to its name! It grows so large in size that it needs the biggest shell it can find on a shallow coral reef for its home.*

Swallows raise their young in a cup of mud glued to a building. To make the nest, the parents collect hundreds of beakfuls of sticky mud, which then dries hard. Before buildings were available, swallows nested on cliffs.

### Endless variety

Animals have made their homes all over the world, from the seabeds to the mountaintops. Some animals find shelter where they can. The moray eel, for example, simply hides in an underwater rock cave. Other animals, like the busy beaver, make such enormous homes that they have completely changed the landscape. Birds can make nests of mud or grass that would amaze any human craftsperson. There are deep, snug **burrows** in the ground for **mammals** and spiders. There are iron-hard fortresses of mud containing thousands— even millions—of fierce insects. Nature's variety is endless, and we humans can learn from it!

5

# Simple Refuges

Tent-building bats live in warm, **tropical** forests, where they feed on fruit. They get their name from their habit of shaping large leaves, like those of the banana tree, into a simple tent. Working from underneath, the bats nibble a leaf near its middle. This causes the edges of the leaf to flop down and make green walls around the bats. The bats then hang from the underside of the leaf, clinging to it with their toes. Often, two or three bats huddle together for warmth. The huge banana leaf, which may measure over 3 feet (90 centimeters) long, protects the bats from the sun, wind, and rain. It also hides them from hunting animals, such as wildcats.

*These bats are hanging upside down in their banana-leaf home in Peru. Many tent-building bats also sleep in caves or tree holes, especially when they are looking after their young, but a leaf tent makes a good shelter.*

## Sharp and shy

Scuba divers on **coral reefs** are always careful not to poke into small caves in rocks or coral. Any one of these dark corners may be home to a moray eel. This long fish has powerful jaws full of razor-sharp **fangs**. By day, the moray hides in its hole, often with just its head showing. It defends the site against any fish that intrudes. At night, the moray eel sneaks among the rocks and coral valleys on the hunt for smaller fish. The moray does nothing to make its home more comfortable. It simply makes do with what it finds.

> *The moray eel's body is just the right shape for sneaking through the twisting, jumbled landscape of a coral reef. Its* **camouflaged** *skin and mouth lining help it blend into the background while it rests during the day.*

# Pack Your Trunk

Leadbeater's possum is a **marsupial,** a kind of **mammal** in which the female nurses her tiny young in a pouch on her belly. This possum lives in the mountain ash forests of Victoria, Australia, the home of some of the world's tallest trees. In the trunks of the oldest trees there are natural holes which make ideal possum nests. All the possum needs to add is some soft bark for bedding. Comfort is important to a Leadbeater's possum, which spends three-quarters of its life in its nest. Sadly, the possum is rare. A fire burned down much of the mountain ash forests in 1939. It will be a long time before the newer trees have enough holes in them to make possum homes.

*Leadbeater's possum is about the size of a gray squirrel. At night it leaves its hole to hunt insects or to lick gum from holes in its tree home.*

## Safely walled in

The hornbill is a large bird with an enormous bill. There are more than 50 hornbill **species** living in the forests of Africa and Asia. The female likes to lay her eggs inside a natural hollow in a tree trunk. Her mate usually finds a hole for her. In order to keep out egg thieves, such as wildcats and eagles, she shapes the entrance hole into a narrow slot. To do this, she sits inside the tree hollow and plasters beakfuls of mud, tree **resin,** or chewed-up food to the edges of the hole to form a wall.

She is soon too large to squeeze out, and her mate must visit her many times each day to feed her. After three or more months, when her young have hatched and have their feathers, the family breaks out. In some species of hornbill, the female loses her flight feathers while in her nest hole. This means that if her mate dies she will starve, for even if she breaks out she cannot fly.

*A male rhinoceros hornbill visits his mate, who is walled up inside her dark nest in the hole of a tree. She and the young will die if he does not come regularly to bring food.*

# Born in a Bank

For a bird that dives into streams to catch fish, a home in the riverbank is perfect. Kingfishers hatch their eggs in a deep **burrow** dug in a steep, sandy bank. Both adults dig the hole. First, the male flies at the bank to stab it with his dagger-like bill. Then the female joins in. Both birds peck at the hole and shovel the loose sand with their feet. The tunnel slopes upwards slightly so that any water drains out easily. It ends in a small, cosy chamber lined with fish bones. The female lays her white eggs in the nest. The male and female take turns sitting on them until they hatch.

The kingfisher's tunnel is usually dug 3 to 6 feet (90 to 180 centimeters) above the water of a river to prevent any risk of flooding. Sometimes kingfishers use the abandoned burrows of other animals.

A platypus leaves its burrow to look for food. When it returns, the tight entrance will squeeze the water from its fur, helping the animal stay dry.

## Duck bills and eggs

It's hard to believe, but three **mammal species** lay eggs! One of these is the duck-billed platypus, which lives in Australian rivers and streams. With its webbed feet and a broad tail, it swims in search of fish, snails, and worms, which it snaps up in its rubbery bill.

The platypus digs two kinds of burrows in the bank. The male and female share one burrow as a shelter until the female is ready to lay her eggs. Then she moves to a much larger burrow of her own. It may run up to 59 feet (18 meters) into the riverbank. She plugs the burrow entrance with earth while she is inside taking care of her young.

# Holes in the Ground

One of the most useful types of **burrow** belongs to the aardvark, a **mammal** of the African woods and grasslands. The aardvark uses its clawed feet to dig into the mounds of ants and termites. Then, it licks up the tiny insects with its long, sticky tongue. Its claws can dig faster than a person can dig with a shovel.

The aardvark, which lives alone, digs many kinds of burrows. Some are shallow, used only for a short rest. Others are deep and twisting, with many tunnels and a nest chamber where a female aardvark looks after her young. Many other animals, including birds, snakes, bats, porcupines, hogs, and wild dogs, hide in aardvark burrows. They do this especially when a fire is raging out of control across the forests or grasslands.

An aardvark emerges at night to look for food. Its main burrow may be up to 40 feet (12 meters) long and have several entrances. It is no wonder other animals try to make their homes in this maze-like warren.

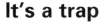

## It's a trap

The trapdoor spider lives in a burrow in the earth. It digs the hole with its **fangs**. Then, it often makes a door from spider **silk** mixed with soil. The spider waits below the door, ready to leap out and pounce on small animals that come it.

*A trapdoor spider usually digs its burrow at a place where insects often walk by. Lurking beneath its door, it senses the vibrations of passing prey.*

There are several **species** of trapdoor spider, and all build different burrows. Some place twigs or lines of silk around the entrance that act as trip wires. When a victim stumbles on a tripwire, out rushes the spider. But trapdoor spiders themselves are sometimes attacked by scorpions and centipedes. So they may build extra burrow chambers or backdoor tunnels as a way of escape.

# Home Share

Whether they hide in holes or sit on webs, most spiders live alone. But a few web-builders live together. In Mexico and the southwestern United States, there live some spiders called Metepeira. Each spider builds its own little web, but this is connected to its neighbors' webs. Together, they build great collections of webs, strung in a silken jumble across several trees.

Why do they do it? Perhaps having a huge web makes it easier to catch food. An insect that flies into one web may bounce off and fly free, but if it is surrounded by webs, the fly is more likely to get trapped. One spider, at least, will not go hungry.

*This great hammock of silk in South America is the work of thousands of **social** spiders, each smaller than a pea. Sharing a web saves them energy and makes it easier to catch insects to eat.*

*Living together is useful for both the shrimp and the goby. The shrimp gets a watchdog, and the goby gets a safe place to hide.*

## Strange bedfellows

Gobies are small fish found on seabeds and riverbeds. They are eaten by many animals, from large fish to dolphins, so they have become good at hiding. The watchman goby shares a **burrow** with a blind shrimp. Although the shrimp is not quite as blind as its name suggests, it cannot see well. Like the goby, it has many enemies. The shrimp spends all its time keeping the sandy burrow in good condition while the goby stands guard outside. All the while, the shrimp rests one of its feelers on the goby. If the goby sees an enemy, it wiggles. At once, the shrimp dashes into its burrow, with the goby following close behind.

Many gobies also like to hide in the holes in natural sponges, which grow on rocks and coral. This protects them from larger fish, which do not like to eat sponges because of their bad taste.

# Stitch and Thatch

The tailor bird is a small Asian bird that builds an unusual nest. The female collects up to three large, green, living leaves. Using her long, sharp bill as a needle, she pierces the edges of each leaf. Then, using spider-web **silk** or plant material like thread, she stitches each leaf into a curled shape. The careful tailor bird ties each end of thread into a ball to keep her stitches from unraveling. When the pocket of leaves is ready she stuffs it with feathers, soft grasses, and fluffy seeds. This makes a strong, waterproof nest that will keep her eggs safe and warm.

*The common tailor bird builds its stitched nest about three feet (one meter) above the ground among the undergrowth. The broad, soft, leathery leaves of many tropical plants are ideal for making strong structures.*

## Wonderful weavers

Some of the most amazing birds' nests are made by weavers. In Africa, several pairs of **social** weavers live together in huge **communal** nests built on trees. They use grasses and twigs to build one big, shared nest.

The birds arrange plant stems so that they point downward, like the straws in the roof of a thatched house. This helps rain run off the nest. The spiky points also keep egg thieves away. Each pair of weavers has its own snug nest chamber lined with feathers or animal fur. Up to 300 pairs may nest together in a single tree!

*Social weavers live together in this huge nest. It is not just a safe place for eggs, but also a cool shelter from the fierce heat of the African sun.*

### Social and family weavers links

Unlike social weavers, some species of weavers live in family groups. They build small nests, woven from grasses, which hang from a branch. Some nests are round, while others are pear-shaped with an entrance tube.

*This male masked weaver builds a beautifully rounded nest for his mate, using slender grass threads.*

# make It with mud

Mud, when it is dried hard by the sun and wind, makes a good building material. Some birds use it to make their nests. Every year, the rufous ovenbird of South America uses a mixture of mud, grasses, and animal dung to build up a large, hollow ball in the crook of a tree branch or a post. This nest looks rather like an old-fashioned clay oven, which explains the bird's name. The nest has thick walls and is so hard that no animal can break it open to reach the eggs or young. For extra safety, the parents build a mud wall halfway across the entrance, leaving a gap only large enough for them to enter.

*The ovenbird's nest is about the size of a football. You can see the little wall that divides the nest into an entrance hall and a secure inner chamber, where the eggs are laid.*

*The magnetic termites of Australia build and live in mounds that look like huge blades pointing toward the sky. Each mound is lined up so that the hot midday sun shines on the narrow, north-facing edges. This means that the inside of the mound does not overheat. The worker termites have a natural sense of which way is north.*

## Termite towns

Termites are small insects that live in huge families known as **colonies.** They have soft, squishy bodies. For protection, they hide underground, inside hollow wood, or in mounds built from **saliva** and soil.

Some termites build huge mounds that are taller than a human. The mounds are full of tunnels that lead from room to room. There are also rooms for eggs, young termites, and the colony's ruling queen and king. There are rooms for storing food and others for waste. There are thousands of termites in each mound.

# Paper and Glue

The hornet is a very large wasp. In the spring, a female hornet starts a family by building a nest. She chews wood and mixes it with her **saliva** to make **pulp**. She molds the pulp into a big, rounded nest that hangs from a branch. She builds egg chambers in the nest. The **larvae** that hatch from the first eggs grow into **workers**. They help her complete the nest.

*A thriving hornet nest can contain many thousands of female worker hornets. They share the duties of building the nest and tending to the larvae. The paper nest is light and surprisingly strong.*

When it is finished, the nest may contain hundreds of the queen's eggs in many layers. An outer layer protects the hornets from the weather and from hungry birds. After summer, the autumn frosts kill off the worker hornets. A few specially produced females will survive the winter to make new nests in the spring.

## Turning over a new leaf

Weaver ants live in the forests of Africa, Asia, and Australia. Like all ants, they live in huge families known as colonies. The weavers are named for their amazing ability to glue leaves together to make homes. Hundreds of ants line up on the edges of a few large leaves in a tree. Using their jaws and claws, they pull the leaves together until the edges touch. Some of the ants then pick up ant larvae in their jaws, and rub the larvae along the leaf edges. From its mouth, each larva oozes a sticky saliva that glues the edges of the leaves together.

*Day after day, weaver ants and larvae glue leaves together, gradually building a vast town of leaf homes in which to live. Where they have to bridge a large gap between leaf edges, the ants form chains of ants linked top to bottom across the gap.*

### Weaver ant and cave swiftlet links

A small bird called the cave swiftlet builds its nest inside large, dark caves. Like the weaver ant grub, the male swiftlet makes lots of sticky saliva. He builds up a gooey cup nest that is stuck to a cave wall. The saliva dries to make a spongy nest that is safe from egg-stealing enemies.

*The cave swiftlet's saliva flows freely, but even so the little bird may take up to two months, working in darkness, to build its nest.*

# Underground Societies

The prairie dog is not a dog at all, but a kind of squirrel that lives in underground **burrows**. The prairie dog, given its name because it barks and wags its tail, lives in towns on the North American prairies.

A prairie-dog town is a maze of burrows. It may be smaller than a backyard garden or stretch for miles in all directions. Each town is divided into neighborhoods called **coteries**. The animals in each coterie are friendly to each other, but drive strangers away. The burrows are deep and long, with entrance holes surrounded by a crater of dirt. This helps prevent flooding. Often there are secret escape tunnels that stop just short of the surface, so they cannot be seen. In an emergency, a prairie dog can dig its way out.

*In every prairie-dog town there are sentries standing guard. When they spot a threat, such as a hungry coyote, the sentries bark a warning. All the animals then dash into the safety of their burrows.*

Mole-rats get cold very easily because they have no fur. They usually huddle together when underground in the burrow.

### Bare burrowers

The naked mole-rat of East Africa lives underground in a family called a **colony.** A king and queen rule the colony, and only they have young. The other animals are just **workers.** The workers take care of the king and queen and dig tunnels with their front teeth. Teams of diggers work together, like miners. When they come across buried roots, they collect them for food.

The unusual lifestyle of naked mole-rats is suited to the place where they live. The land is very hot and dry, yet the air down in the burrows stays cool and moist. And the ground is so hard that a single mole-rat simply could not dig a burrow alone. Living together, mole-rats achieve more than they could on their own.

# Building Big

The beaver is a giant **rodent,** a relative of rats, mice, and squirrels. Beaver families live on a lake or river. The beavers use their teeth to cut down trees and drag them to the water. They pile up the wood to build a **dam** across the flowing water. Soon, the blocked water rises behind the dam, making a deep, wide lake. In the lake, the beavers pile more timber in a heap. They chew out the middle of the heap to make a hollow. This home is called a lodge. Inside the lodge, the hollow is warm and dry. Surrounded by water, the beavers are safe from bears and wolves.

*Beavers not only build with wood, they also eat it, especially the leaves, twigs and bark. They heap up more wood to make a winter food store not far from the lodge. They can reach the store even when the lake is iced over.*

*The hamerkop's nest looks messy, as though it were built in a hurry, but it is very strong. The roof is so sturdy that a human could stand on it, and the structure lasts for years and years.*

## Super stack

The hamerkop is an African bird which builds its enormous nest in a tree near a river. A pair of hamerkops build with anything they can find, from sticks and reeds to bones. First, they heap up a thick platform. Then, they build up the walls and make a thick roof overhead. Finally, they plaster the inside walls with mud. The nest, which takes about six weeks to build, may measure six feet (almost two meters) across.

The hamerkops build a new nest the following year, and new animals move into the old, empty home. Sparrows, eagle owls, geese, snakes, lizards, and bees have all made themselves comfortable in empty hamerkop homes.

# Homes in Harsh Places

The desert tortoise lives in the hot, dry, southwestern United States, where it spends more than nine-tenths of its life in a **burrow**. A burrow keeps the tortoise comfortable and hides it from hunters, such as coyotes, kit foxes, ravens, and golden eagles.

Desert tortoises usually have two or more burrows. In one, they sleep through the cold winter. This burrow is up to 29.5 feet (9 meters) long. The tunnel roof is often curved to match the tortoise's shell shape. A shorter burrow is used for the summer, when the ground outside is too hot for much activity. After a sudden summer rainfall, plants bloom in the desert. Then the tortoise comes up to feed, but soon it creeps down into its burrow again.

*The desert tortoise has strong, spade-like forelimbs it uses to dig its burrow in the desert sand.*

## Against the flow

Caddis flies are flying insects that look like moths. They lay their eggs in rivers or lakes, and the worm-like **larvae** that hatch live in the water. The larvae spin **silk** from their mouths. Some use the silk to knit a jacket made from sand grains, pieces of water plant, broken shells, or twigs. The jacket helps them resist strong water currents and hide from fish.

A caddis fly larva molts, or sheds its skin, several times as it grows. Each time, it must spin and build a new home. Other caddis fly larvae build a small home, rather like a turtle's shell, on the surface of a stone. Some fix the shell to the stone, but others carry it from place to place.

*Many caddis fly **species** form their **pupae** inside a tube of fragments, just like the tube they lived in as larvae. Here, an adult caddis fly is finally emerging from its pupal home.*

# Fact File

The bee hummingbird, which lives in the Caribbean, is the world's smallest bird, just 1.9 to 2.4 inches (5 to 6 cm) long. Its nest, fixed to a leaf or plant stem, is a tiny woven cup of spiders' webs and bark no bigger than half a walnut shell!

White storks are big birds that like to nest up high. So it's no surprise they often choose a chimney pot! In parts of Europe it is considered good luck to have a stork nest on your chimney.

Humans aren't the only ones that make their homes look pretty. Bowerbirds of Australia and New Guinea are champion decorators. The males do this to attract females to their nest. The satin bowerbird collects feathers, flowers, shells, and even human trash, usually in shades of blue. He even gathers blueberries and chews them, then paints the nest with the berry juice. Other bowerbirds collect shiny objects, like aluminum foil or candy wrappers.

The acorn barnacle is related to crabs and lobsters. As a young animal it swims freely, but later it settles in one place. Then it produces a strong glue it uses to stick its head to a rock. Some barnacles choose a mobile home—the bottom of a ship or a whale's skin. A large ship may carry several tons of barnacles. There, the barnacle builds a shell of limestone around its body. In order to feed, the barnacle stretches its long, feathery legs out into the water to trap tiny pieces of food that float by.

Most crabs grow a hard plate of armor, called a carapace, over their soft, inner body. The hermit crab, however, does not. This animal borrows an empty seashell for a home. Its soft **abdomen** is specially coiled in order to fit such a shell. As the hermit crab grows, it must shed the shell from time to time and find a larger home.

The largest prairie-dog town ever known ranged over 25,096 square miles (65,000 square km)–about half the area of Great Britain. It was probably home to about 400 million animals!

The female potter wasp uses mud to build tiny, jug-shaped nest pots. She lays one egg in each pot. Before she seals the jug shut with a mud lid, she stuffs it with caterpillars or spiders. These will be food for the wasp grub when it hatches. When the grub has grown into a wasp, it breaks out of the jug that has been its home.

# Glossary

**abdomen**   back section of an insect, spider, or crab

**burrow**   home made by digging a tunnel in the ground or in a plant. There is usually a living area at the end.

**camouflage**   anything that hides an animal from its enemies or prey

**colony**   group of animals that live together, share food, and work for the common good. The animals are usually related.

**communal**   belonging to a large group of animals or to several families of animals

**coral reef**   colony made up of thousands of tiny animals that build a hard skeleton around their soft bodies. They share food. Coral lives in shallow, sunlit seas, where their skeletons form reefs.

**coterie**   community of prairie dogs that are friendly to each other and live together in a single neighborhood that is part of a bigger town

**dam**   blockage across a river that causes the water to rise up behind it

**fang**   tooth shaped like a needle or a knife

**instinct**   knowledge of how to do something without having been taught

**larva** (more than one are called larvae)   young form of an insect that does not yet look like its parents

**mammal**   warm-blooded, furry animal that feeds its young on milk produced by the mother

**marsupial**   mammal that carries its young in a pouch

**pulp**   mashed mixture of, for example, water and wood

**pupa** (more than one are called pupae)    stage in an insect's life between larva and adult

**resin**    sticky liquid produced in a tree. Many animals eat tree gums and resins.

**rodent**    mammal with ever-growing front teeth that are used to gnaw hard food

**saliva**    liquid made in an animal's mouth

**silk**    liquid, produced by many insect larvae and spiders, which hardens on contact with air to make a very strong thread

**social**    describes an animal that lives with other animals of its own kind in order to share food or shelter, or to form a common defense against enemies

**species**    type of living thing

**tropical**    describes hot regions of the world where the sun is directly overhead for part of the year

**worker**    among social insects and naked mole-rats, a special form of individual that lives only to work for the good of a colony

# More Books to Read

Fredericks, Anthony D. and Sneed B. Collard. *Amazing Animals: Nature's Most Incredible Creatures.* Chanhassen, Minn.: Creative Publishing International, 2000.

Squire, Ann O. *Animal Homes.* Danbury, Conn.: Children's Press, 2001.

Winnett, David A. *Animals and Their Homes.* White Plains, N.Y.: Dale Seymour Publications, 1999.

# Index

aardvarks 12
acorn barnacles 29

bats 6, 12
bears 24
beavers 4, 5, 24
bee hummingbirds 28
bees 25
blind shrimp 15
bowerbirds 28

caddis flies 27
cave swiftlets 21
centipedes 13
coral reefs 7
coyotes 26
crabs 29

desert tortoises 26
duck-billed platypuses 11

eagle owls 25

geese 25
gobies 15
golden eagles 26

hamerkops 25
hermit crabs 4, 29
hogs 12
hornbills 9
hornets 4, 20

kingfishers 10
kit foxes 26

Leadbeater's possums 8
lizards 25
lobsters 29

masked weavers 17
moray eels 5, 7

naked mole-rats 23

porcupines 12
potter wasps 29
prairie dogs 22, 29

ravens 26
rufous ovenbirds 18

scorpions 13
shrimp 15
snakes 12, 25
sparrows 25
spiders 5, 13, 14, 28, 29
swallows 5

tailor birds 16
tent-building bats 6
termites 19
trapdoor spiders 13

weaver ants 21
weaver birds 17
white storks 28
wild dogs 12
wolves 24